It Is Written

It Is Written: Freedom Farm Journal
Copyright © 2013

All Rights Reserved.
No part of this book may be reproduced in any form without permission in writing from the author or publisher.

Scripture taken from the Holy Bible New Living Translation (NLT). Copyright © 1996, 2004, 2007 by Tyndale House Foundation. Used by permission. All rights reserved.

ISBN: 978-1-935256-30-4

Ledge Press
PO Box 1652
Boone, NC 28607
www.ledgepress.com
ledgepress@gmail.com

Freedom Farm Ministries

Message and Purpose

Freedom Farm Ministries, located in the beautiful Blue Ridge Mountains of North Carolina, was founded with a purposeful vision to provide men a way out of bondage to alcohol and drug addiction through the Person and Power of Jesus Christ. The three-fold plan for this freedom includes:

- Providing a Christian center of refuge for men who are desperate and ready to have God change them.
- Providing a Christian drug and alcohol restoration program to a select few men looking for a way to grow as disciples of Jesus Christ. Located in a rural setting, this program teaches, through intense focus on scripture, how to be eternally free from the bondage of addiction.
- Providing a Christian drug and alcohol program geared toward providing men the counseling and community support to successfully transition from the recovery stage, to life back in the world, but not of the world.

Overall, Freedom Farm Ministries is a community, such as the early church where openness and honesty are valued, sharing is practiced, and study of Scripture forms the basis for decisions.

Safe House

The Safe House, aptly named the Arms of Jesus (AOJ), offers immediate shelter to men wanting to break free of the bondage of addiction but lacking a safe place to stay. Here they become aware of a better way to find peace and contentment. The Safe House program currently serves up to twenty men.

Set in rural Ashe County on a 36 acre farm, the Safe House provides nurture and love for men often in physical, emotional, and spiritual pain. The first few days are spent getting better physically, but soon the men begin to fully participate in the Safe House activities. With balanced, healthy food and a Christian environment, men bond together, having morning devotions and light Bible studies as a daily routine. During the day, a light work schedule is followed, often working with the farm animals or helping to maintain the Freedom Farm Ministries' facilities.

Weekly individual coaching and mentoring is provided as well as assistance in determining the best "next step" for each man. Assistance is provided with obtaining letters for court and probation issues. Men prepare for the move to our Restoration House. The Freedom Farm Ministries year-long Discipleship program begins with the Safe House.

Restoration – Second Stage

Thirty miles from Boone NC, there are 18 acres of beautiful rolling mountains with trout streams and several springs.

This serene location is the site of the Christian recovery program (Restoration House).

The goal at Restoration House is to present the Lord Jesus Christ as personal savior – the only one who can free men of their bondage. As God does His wonderful miracle of salvation, staff will continue to lead each man into a personal relationship with Jesus Christ.

Self-study, as well as daily devotions and group classes, is packed into 40 days in a regimented and pure environment. No TV, no tobacco products, and very little time away from the cabin allow a man to concentrate on his past, present, and future.

With a capacity of six to eight men, each Restoration House offers an intense recovery program geared to each individual man. The specialized program for each man is designed to "go deep" and deal with conditions preventing him from true freedom in Christ. Men enter Restoration House through the Safe House program having made a commitment to the year-long FFM <u>Discipleship Program</u> (DLC).

Discipleship Living Center (DLC)
Freedom Farm's Discipleship Living Center (DLC) offers men recovering from alcohol and/or drug addiction a safe and challenging environment where they can grow in their relationship with Jesus Christ. Its mission is to lead them to become disciples,

able to live in the world without drugs, and to eventually be able to pass on to others what they have received. DLC furthers each man's spiritual growth in three areas:

- In understanding Jesus Christ as he is described and presented in the Bible
- In trusting Jesus Christ with all the details of life
- And in obeying Jesus Christ in all areas of life.

Founded in September 2006 with two men, the first DLC location provided a safe place for men to live for a nominal fee. Since that time four additional houses have opened to meet the need. DLC allows men to live in a Christian community, interacting with other men who have had similar experiences. In each "home" six to eight men live and study, pray, cook & clean together under the direction of a "house man" and the DLC Director. The typical length of stay is six to eight months.

Men are assisted in finding responsible, safe employment in the local community and helped to save money for a fresh start. They are taught to grow strong so they won't fall to the temptations of their old life. DLC provides pastoral counseling for those who are trying to understand broken relationships in their lives, transportation for those without a driver's license, and vehicles for those with a license in order to get to and from employment.

Freedom Farm Ministries History

Founded in 2006 by executive director Robbie Collie and his wife Rita, Freedom Farm Ministries was a direct result of a life and heart changed by the peace which true release from addiction provides.

Freedom Farm is a non-profit 501(c)(3) ministry built completely with the intention of helping men and their families find the freedom gained by growing in a life centered in Jesus Christ. Hundreds of men have already received that new life, and many have renewed health and reputations. Men have been reunited with family, but most importantly have gained restored spirits and relationships with the Father.

You can support Freedom Farm Ministries in two ways:
First, you can pray for us. Pray for the men in the program. This is the most important way you can support us.

You can support with your donations. Freedom Farm Ministries is a faith-funded ministry. By faith, a majority of our support comes from churches, friends, and those whose lives have been personally impacted by chemical addiction.

Each gift is a blessing and we are regularly blessed by those who are "recurring givers" through our online giving program.

You can donate by using the Give Online button found on our website www.freedomfarmministries.org. Your contribution means that Freedom Farm Ministries is able to provide Christian recovery and restoration to men in bondage to chemical addiction. Your gift today provides hope and relief for tomorrow as you join with us in proclaiming His "freedom to captives." Isaiah 61:1, Luke 4:18

Freedom Farm Ministries
P O Box 153, Boone NC 28607
828.964.2914 (office) • 336.385.9747 (fax)
Robbie Collie, Executive Director

Oswald Chambers

The Surrendered Life

I have been crucified with Christ… (Galatians 2:20)

To become one with Jesus Christ, a person must be willing not only to give up sin, but also to render his whole way of looking at things. Being born again by the Spirit of God means that we must first be willing to let go before we can grasp something else. The first thing we must surrender is all of our pretense or deceit. What our Lord wants us to present to Him is not our goodness, honesty, or our efforts to do better, but real solid sin. Actually, that is all He can take from us. And what He gives us in exchange for our sin is real solid righteousness. But we must surrender all pretense that we are anything, and give up all our claims of even being worthy of God's consideration.

Once we have done that, the Spirit of God will show us what we need to surrender next. Along each step of this process, we will have to give up our claims to our rights to ourselves. Are we willing to surrender our grasp on all that we possess our desires, and everything else in our lives? Are we ready to be identified with the death of Jesus Christ?

We will suffer a sharp painful disillusionment before we fully surrender. When people really see themselves as the Lord sees them, it is not the terrible offensive sin of the flesh that shocks them, but the awful nature of the pride of their own hearts opposing Jesus Christ. When they see themselves in the light of the Lord, the shame, horror, and desperate conviction hit home for them.

If you are faced with the question of whether or not to surrender, make a determination to go on through the crisis, surrendering all that you have and all that you are to Him. And God will equip you to do all that He requires of you.

"My Utmost For His Highest," 1992 by Oswald Chambers Publications Association, Ltd.

Mark A.

James 1:19
Understand this, my dear brothers and sisters: You must all be quick to listen, slow to speak, and slow to get angry.

This verse is very important to me. I have always struggled with speaking my opinion too quickly based on what I perceive as right or wrong without questioning God's position. This has been a key lesson in separating myself from living by worldly standards. Today, I try to listen more than I speak, asking what God would want me to do or say. I must live by God's will and not my own.

Joe H.

Matthew 16:25
If you try to hang on to your life, you will lose it. But if you give up your life for My sake, you will save it.

I am reminded of the times in my life when I tried to hold onto myself or my selfish desires. I was thinking that these things gave me purpose or would give me life. But I think what God sees is me holding onto death and the things that would never bring me happiness or a real life. Once I stop chasing after worldly things and those things that come from selfish desires, I can begin to build a <u>relationship</u> with Christ. I will begin to walk with Him and listen to His voice. This leads me to finding my true life. I love the verse that follows this one, "What will it benefit a man if he gains the whole world yet forfeits his own soul? What will a man give in exchange for his life?" The word "forfeit" reminds me of a game where the team just gives up; they don't even put up a fight to win. How many times have I just given up and not even put up a fight? So many times I trade the life Christ has for me for a life of nothing. I don't want to live a life like that. And I realize that this is an everyday thing. I need Christ to do that. The only way I find the true and meaningful life is in Christ. Today, I want to put up a fight. Amen.

Dan A.

2 Corinthians 12:9
Each time He said, "My grace is all you need. My power works best in weakness." So now I am glad to boast about my weaknesses, so that the power of Christ can work through me.

I have been brought to my knees in humiliation, humbleness and desperation through the weaknesses of my life: life's failures, addictions, a lustful nature. It is true: He whose is, is greater than I. Only in my failures as a man have I experienced the riches of God's glory given to me freely through His grace. His grace is truly sufficient. His grace allows for a supernatural exchange of my sinful self; death deserving of His holy, perfect righteousness filled with abundant life. I praise God for allowing me to see the failure of living in my own strength. I praise God for my weaknesses so that I can experience His sovereignty, power and grace.

Mark A.

Sweet Surrender

It is written:
James 1:19-22
[19] Understand this, my dear brothers and sisters: You must all be quick to listen, slow to speak, and slow to get angry. [20] Human anger does not produce the righteousness God desires. [21] So get rid of all the filth and evil in your lives, and humbly accept the word God has planted in your hearts, for it has the power to save your souls. [22] But don't just listen to God's word. You must do what it says. Otherwise, you are only fooling yourselves.

Inspiration flooded me as I read these verses from James. This flood of inspiration propelled my fight to leave my drug addiction along with the lifestyle that goes with it. Before my personal relationship with God through Christ, my life and my thoughts were in a state of total confusion. I realize now that the devil had me right where he wanted me. I didn't even see it. I resented everyone and everything around me except money and drugs. When family members or friends confronted me about my problems, I would start yelling and swearing to the point where they would leave me alone. This is how I got what I wanted—isolation. I did not even want to see my kids, much less anyone else. The only thing I was interested in was satisfying my addiction. I was truly at the end of my life on earth. I felt sure I was headed to hell. 6/18/12 was the day I decided to have complete faith in God. This is the day I surrendered my life to Him and gave myself back to Him. It was the day I realized I was not dead. No drug or high could match this. This was not a worldly feeling but something "supernatural." It had only one source-- my Father, the Lord God Himself. From that moment, I truly wanted to follow in the footsteps of Jesus Christ, even though I felt I could never do that. But it became my goal to give my best in this new life. I have no idea why I became addicted to drugs and chose to live a life of sin. I don't even understand what God has in store for me next, but I do know He is in the details and that's good enough for me. I realize everything that happens does not always seem good, but everything that happens is for the good. I know if I die today I'm going to heaven. That's the best gift I could ever ask for or even imagine. "Praise God."

Steve C.

Content in the Lord!

2 Corinthians 5:17
This means that anyone who belongs to Christ has become a new person. The old life is gone; a new life has begun!

I can see this verse slowly manifesting itself in my life. The change is occurring for me in many areas of my life. The conviction of the Holy Spirit was the first thing that I noticed about this new creation. I am no longer free to sin. Sin no longer has the appeal to me that it once did in the world. I now feel less and less a part of this world. I am longing more and more for a close relationship with my heavenly Father. What used to be of value to me has lost its appeal.

Kyle A.

I Thessalonians 4:11-12
¹¹ Make it your goal to live a quiet life, minding your own business and working with your hands, just as we instructed you before. ¹² Then people who are not Christians will respect the way you live, and you will not need to depend on others.

Christ is the only one I should depend on or can depend on for what matters. I've never had the relationship with Christ that has allowed me to abide in his strength and wisdom to fulfill God's plan for me on my own. I've had to rely on family and others to supplement my lack of progress. How do we become independent of others, you may ask? Paul suggests it is only through Christ. He even gives three ways to become more independent from others and dependent on Christ. "We should make it our ambition…" Devoted to living in the light becomes my ambition. Even when I fail to live in the light, my ambition is to be devoted to this. "Live a quiet life, with your own hands." My purpose becomes to follow Him, to be devoted to Him and His way of living. By my example, I can be a light to the World. This makes it possible for those who are non-believers to see us live, see our walk and become inspired. If I am following Christ, then those who do not know Christ can see Him and hear Him in me.

Dan A.

John 6:29
Jesus told them, "This is the only work God wants from you: Believe in the one He has sent."

I've struggled in the past about how to serve and love God with all my heart. What do I do? What is my work? Through the truth of this scripture, I am continuously set free from an old mindset that whispers that my actions determine who I am or what my identity is but we are simply called to believe: believe that Christ paid it all on the cross and it is finished; believe that the only way that I am made whole and clean is by the blood of Christ; believe the word of God more than my past experiences, failures, successes or even my own understanding. God calls me to simply believe and just be. When this truth settles in my heart, all feelings of inadequacy lose their power over me. Now I am seized by a desire to become the person God created me to be.

Jeff S.

Galatians 3:23
Before the way of faith in Christ was available to us, we were placed under guard by the law. We were kept in protective custody, so to speak, until the way of faith was revealed.

What an impact words from Scripture can have. Before I found Christ I was a prisoner to my own self! I was trapped in the law of my own punishment. I wasn't ready to let go until I understood what Christ Jesus did for me. I surrendered. I opened my heart. I died to myself. My faith was revealed to me. Today, my faith is growing bigger and becoming stronger as He walks with me.

Steve C.

Content in the Lord!

Galatians 2:20
My old self has been crucified with Christ. It is no longer I who live, but Christ lives in me. So I live in this earthly body by trusting in the Son of God, who loved me and gave Himself for me.

Again, the old sinner is dying away. This scripture is what I can stand firm on. Yes, there is still life in the flesh but there's a difference in me. Christ lives in me. I have faith in the Son of God. I now know where love in my heart comes from. He loved me first. He died for this sinner, who is crossing over from darkness. A life of no meaning or purpose is moving to the light. Truth, purpose, love, joy. Freedom. I am being forgiven and developing the ability to forgive.

James F.

It Is Written

Joshua 1:9
This is my command—be strong and courageous! Do not be afraid or discouraged. For the Lord your God is with you wherever you go."

Since the first day I read this verse it has helped me. I arrived at Freedom Farm in desperate need of a fresh start on life. I had forgotten how to live my life. The trials of my life up to this point made me realize how much I needed Jesus. Joshua 1:9 helped me face my addiction of pain killers and alcohol head-on. Joshua reminded me that no matter how tough life gets, God will be with me through it all. For a long time, I was angry with God and scared that I was on my own through life. I felt discouraged all the time with the things that were happening to me. I couldn't figure out why I felt like I wasn't getting anywhere. I had worked so hard to get where I was in my life. I was successful in my teaching and coaching profession. But confusion became a reality. Eventually, I figured it out—I had not surrendered my life to God. I had not given Him everything in my life. I had failed to give Him all the glory for my success. This verse made me realize that I need to be strong in my faith in God and be courageous and live for Jesus Christ each day.

Mike F.

The Power of Prayer

James 5:16
Confess your sins to each other and pray for each other so that you may be healed. The earnest prayer of a righteous person has great power and produces wonderful results.

A lot can be said for good communication. Staying connected is important for husbands, sons, brothers, fathers, and men of God. This may seem obvious when it comes to family, but a lot of new Christians often underestimate the importance of this simple application in our new lives in Christ. How can we expect to stay connected to God if we never talk to Him? How can we know His will if we never ask Him what it is? God wants to use us, but we have to take the time out of our day to commune with Him before His Holy Spirit can work through us. The Apostle Paul says to "Pray without ceasing" (I Thess. 5:17). You see, prayer is more than just an endless recitation of "Father this" and "God that." He wants us to speak from the heart, not give a speech. You don't need to impress God, you just need to give Him a call. As His children, we have an open line of communication with the Father that is unrivaled by any "high speed connections," DSL, or cell phone reception. He is always listening and He always cares. Why don't you take some time, hit your knees, and tell your Father about your day.

Kevin E.

Some of the Secrets of God

It is written:
1 Corinthians 4:1-2
So look at Apollos and me as mere servants of Christ who have been put in charge of explaining God's mysteries. Now, a person who is put in charge as a manager must be faithful.

God called and called but I would not heed the calling. The power I was seeking was the power to control; the power of wealth and to be served, not to serve others. Time after time, I would gain this power only to lose it for it wasn't of God but of the world. Then Jesus revealed Himself to me as God. He touched my spirit, He opened my eyes and He opened my heart to the truth, and He gave me a vision. This vision was not about me, but about Him and His unfailing, unwavering love. He surrounded me with His people and is teaching me secrets that only followers of Christ can know.…And now I have a mission. It's no longer I who live, but Christ that lives in me. He's given me a measure of faith to share and to serve and to bless others.…Thank you Father God. Are you proving yourself faithful?

Curt D.

It Is Written

Ephesians 2:22
Through Him you Gentiles are also being made part of this dwelling where God lives by His Spirit.

This verse is important to me because it affirms that I am worthy of God. It tells me that I am a work in progress. But God will make me into a temple or building deserving of keeping His word. When I first came to Freedom Farm, I wasn't sure that God's grace would extend to me because I was such a failure as a person. I was an addict and alcoholic, liar, cheater, thief and generally a self-absorbed person. Now, God shows me daily how to prove my worth and be a vessel in which He dwells.

Jonathan S.

Psalm 40:1-3
¹ I waited patiently for the Lord to help me, and He turned to me and heard my cry.
² He lifted me out of the pit of despair, out of the mud and the mire. He set my feet on solid ground and steadied me as I walked along.
³ He has given me a new song to sing, a hymn of praise to our God. Many will see what He has done and be amazed. They will put their trust in the Lord.

This passage is a great reminder of how God rescued me from the destruction of my addiction that plagued me for years. My addiction put me in bondage for a long time. Just as it seemed all hope had been lost, God heard my cries and lifted me out of that pit of despair. He has lifted me up, putting my feet back on solid ground. Now, having Jesus Christ as the foundation in my life, I feel I have stability once again. Hopefully, others will be able to see what God has done for me and maybe they, too, will place their trust in Him as I have. With these things, I believe I can move forward with great confidence and joy to live a successful Christian life.

Eric A.

It Is Written

Psalm 23:4-6

Even when I walk through the darkest valley, I will not be afraid, for you are close beside me. Your rod and your staff protect and comfort me. You prepare a feast for me in the presence of my enemies. You honor me by anointing my head with oil. My cup overflows with blessings. Surely your goodness and unfailing love will pursue me all the days of my life, and I will live in the house of the Lord forever.

God has loved and sustained me even in the bad times. Psalm 23:4-6 gives me the courage to be strong even in the face of evil. When I am down, I know that God has a place for me in this life and the next. Now I have hope that I did not have during the bad times. God gives me assurance that His comfort, through His Word, will never leave me and will always be available to me. Knowing that God has never left me makes me want to be a better man for Christ. During the bad times, it is very easy to forget to go to Christ. Sometimes I even turned my back on Him for the addiction. Going for the "feel good" instead of relying on Christ for a spiritual "feel good." I know that God is a merciful God. I know that through the blood of Jesus, my sins are forgiven.

Curt D.

Micah 6:8
No, O people, the Lord has told you what is good, and this is what He requires of you: to do what is right, to love mercy, and to walk humbly with your God.

Here are instructions for how to live my life after Freedom Farm and out in the real world. If I maintain my faith, help my fellow man, and am just, merciful and humble in all my actions, I will be a success. Not only to my God, but to my family, friends and church. God has shown me all that is good. All He requires of me is to be humble and include justice and mercy in my day to day thinking. (And just to believe in Him).

Zack C.

Psalm 34:18
The Lord is close to the brokenhearted; He rescues those whose spirits are crushed.

I identify with this verse because it reminds me the Lord is closest to those who are hurt and broken and saves us who are at the end of ourselves with nowhere to go. A strong use of language referring to a broken spirit – crushed – that's the men coming into Freedom Farm Ministries.

Jason F.

It Is Written

Matthew 7:1
Do not judge others, and you will not be judged.

Throughout my life, I've traveled down two dead end roads. I continued to follow sin for happiness without ever reaching it, causing chaos everywhere I turned. Then the days grew longer and life became harder to deal with. People judged me for all those roads I once traveled on and I started to see. While sitting in a cell block in prison, a Christian brother showed me this verse. He then explained to me that as a Christian, we are not allowed to judge one another. This verse has allowed me to enter into society and only care about what God thinks. He has guided me back into society with a new life where I have been accepted. He also put me on a new road which has led me to Freedom Farm. This wonderful new family has overwhelmed me without faulting me for my past.

Curt D.

Micah 6:8
No, O people, the Lord has told you what is good, and this is what He requires of you: to do what is right, to love mercy, and to walk humbly with your God.

These words remind me that all of the good in my life has come to me because of the grace of God. In return, I should strive to uphold justice, show mercy to my fellow man, and to remain humble in all that I do. Out of all the perfections that we aspire to in order to be more Christ-like, these remind me of the insignificance of myself and to let Jesus' light shine through me in my actions.

Zack C.

Isaiah 40:31
But those who trust in the Lord will find new strength.
They will soar high on wings like eagles.
They will run and not grow weary. They will walk and not faint.

These words speak of how stillness and patience in the Lord results in his new strength that He will give us if we stay obedient. Wait on his blessing, fight the good fight of faith, be steady in the Lord and He will reveal himself at exactly the right moment.

Wesley W.

It Is Written

Jeremiah 29:11-13
"For I know the plans I have for you," says the Lord. "They are plans for good and not for disaster, to give you a future and a hope. In those days when you pray, I will listen. If you look for Me wholeheartedly, you will find Me."

For as long as I can remember, my parents have told me God has a plan for me. God has a plan for everyone and will never lead us astray. Everything we do, we must do for God's glory. I need to trust in God and lean on Him in everything I do. All my life I heard my parents say these things to me, and most of my life I didn't believe them. It's amazing to look back in my life and see how God has used the dark, negative experiences and trials in my life to bring me closer to Him. Jesus's death was not the result of a panicking cosmological engineer. The cross wasn't a tragic surprise. The death of the Son of God was anything but an unexpected peril. No, it was part of a plan. It was a calculated choice. The cross was drawn into the original blueprint. God's plan is always fulfilled.

Mike F.

It Is Written

James 1:8
Their loyalty is divided between God and the world, and they are unstable in everything they do.

"From Christian to Atheist and Back Again"

I was saved at the tender age of eight. I was raised in church and knew the conviction of sin and that only Christ could save me from eternal damnation.

As my life progressed into adolescence and I was unable to live a 'good' Christian life and I became angry with God. I became accusatory towards Him for everything that went wrong in my life. When I went away to college, I adopted the principles of existentialism and quickly realized that the only way I could let go of my hatred for God was to cease believing in Him.

For a time, I had inner peace. I met my wife of ten years and we had three beautiful children, all of which were taught that "there is no God." My alcoholism began to spiral out of control. I had a grasp on morality, but my spiritual self was rotting from the inside. I was out of control; drinking from daylight to dark and abusing any drug I could get my hands on. My wife, though she loved me, could not tolerate my destructive behavior anymore.

She filed for divorce and I was devastated. I slipped further into addiction. I didn't want to live. I hated my life.

Psalm 14:1
Only fools say in their hearts, "There is no God." They are corrupt, and their actions are evil; not one of them does good!

After a thirty day stint in jail, I committed myself to the will of God and surrendered to His plan for my life; without conditions and without my fingers crossed behind my back. If it was His will that my marriage be reconciled, then so be it. If not, then I would still praise Him. Today, I am sober and more spiritually aware of God's love and compassion than I have ever been. I don't fret for tomorrow and I take my burdens to Christ. Thank God that even an atheist can come back to the Father and be loved unconditionally.

_____

_____

_____

_____

_____

_____

_____

_____

Anthony B.

It Is Written

2 Corinthians 4:4
Satan, who is the god of this world, has blinded the minds of those who don't believe. They are unable to see the glorious light of the Good News. They don't understand this message about the glory of Christ, who is the exact likeness of God.

True order and safety for humans will only come with the return of our Savior, Jesus Christ. Until then, our job as Christians is to educate the rest of mankind that Satan is out to destroy us for all eternity. We must remember for ourselves and show others by our life that there is only one way to win the battle on earth. That is, to entrust everything to God, have Jesus pay our sin debt, and allow the Holy Spirit to guide our every step thereafter. Christ won the war for us on the cross, why not live out our gratitude on earth by defeating Satan and his demons in the spiritual battles we can win through Christ today… every day?

Eric T.

It Is Written

Romans 8:28
And we know that God causes everything to work together for the good of those who love God and are called according to His purpose for them.

This has been my life verse for a long time, and it has given me hope because God can take all the evil and chaos and sin in my life and put a positive value on it. He has done this for me in so many ways at so many different times, and He still does. It has also produced a tremendous testimony that I can share with other people (especially the lost souls) in order to give them hope. Whenever my faith begins to falter due to trials and tribulations, I can look back at all the terrible situations that God has delivered me from and it renews my faith and hope. Romans 8:28 gives me assurance that God is constantly at work behind the scenes from the mightiest of [our emotional] works down to the smallest detail.

Paul E.

Romans 8:39
No power in the sky above or in the earth below—indeed, nothing in all creation will ever be able to separate us from the love of God that is revealed in Christ Jesus our Lord.

This verse reminds me that I could never do anything to cause God to stop loving me. It also reminds me of how much He loves me because it says, "in Christ Jesus our Lord." It is through Jesus that I can come boldly to the throne of God.

Curt D.

Psalm 46:10
Be still, and know that I am God! I will be honored by every nation. I will be honored throughout the world.

These are words of exhortation to remain quiet, meditate, and fellowship with my God. This has been difficult to do since my pride, ego and self-worth compel me to constantly "run the show." In Hebrew, what has been interpreted to mean "stop moving" actually loosely means "stop striving." As such, I remind myself to do both, which is calming and also allows me to accept God's direction. I let Jesus "take the wheel", if you will.

James F.

Hebrews 4:16

So let us come boldly to the throne of our gracious God. There we will receive his mercy, and we will find grace to help us when we need it most.

When I came to Freedom Farm, I was in a desperate time in my life. I needed God more than ever. When I read this verse, I realized that God was a forgiving God and if I came to Him with love and confidence, He would grant me mercy. I knew He would give me grace every day as long as I gave Him all my confidence and my trust.

Paul E.

1 Corinthians 15:22

Just as everyone dies because we all belong to Adam, everyone who belongs to Christ will be given new life.

This verse means that Adam brought sin into the world, which causes death, but through Christ I live forever. Abundant life here on earth and eternally with Him in heaven. Though I still sin, it has no power over me. Because of the atonement of the blood of Jesus, my sins are wiped away.

Frank J.

It Is Written

Matthew 11:28-30
Then Jesus said, "Come to Me, all of you who are weary and carry heavy burdens, and I will give you rest. Take My yoke upon you. Let Me teach you, because I am humble and gentle at heart, and you will find rest for your souls. For My yoke is easy to bear, and the burden I give you is light."

These verses are the first verses in scripture that really seemed to speak to me personally. All my life, I seemed to have been carrying some burden of some sort and I really did not know how to let go of it. All the things I had tried over the years (sex, alcohol, drugs, etc.) only seemed to lift the burden for a short while. The problem was the burden became heavier and heavier.

Jesus says in this passage that He is gentle and meek. This is the exact opposite of the way of the world. Jesus asks me to join Him and become one with Him and He will help me carry whatever it is in life that I have to bear. I was so tired of feeling alone and afraid that when I first read these verses, they immediately got my attention. This passage tells me that all I have to do is let go of whatever it is that I am holding onto and give it to Jesus. He is the Great Burden Bearer and walks with me and helps me carry my load each day. I just have to surrender and give it to Him.

James F.

Jeremiah 29:13
If you look for Me wholeheartedly, you will find Me.

This verse really helped me when I went to Restoration. I was, at that time, seeking God and His wisdom. I was seeking the confidence I needed to survive the struggles of everyday life. It gives me the hope and faith I need in my daily walk to put all my trust in Him and know everything will be okay. If I seek Him each day with all my heart, He will provide.

Cory M.

Since I've been at Restoration, I've noticed a change in myself. Although, I've realized that I'm still holding onto some of my old habits, like lying. I think lying is easy and stays with me because I've lied almost my whole life. No one showed me grace or mercy for telling the truth—so I kept on lying. Also, I see that I need to start trusting in God more, rather than myself. If I would have trusted in Him in this situation, then I would have felt more comfortable telling the truth no matter what the outcome was. Through this situation, I've learned that I need to stop trying to take control of my life and let God have control for once. Also, I need to have more faith that God will allow people to show me mercy, love and respect even though I may have done wrong.

Mike F.

Emotional Baggage

It is written:
Psalm 103:12
He has removed our sins as far from us as the east is from the west.

I have been an addict for almost twenty years. While I have had brief periods of sobriety throughout my life, I have struggled with relapse after relapse. Every time I think I have completely surrendered to Jesus, I find the remains of emotional baggage overwhelming me. If we let the guilt and shame of our past lives invade our minds, we will have a continually restless spirit. This is not the life Christ intends for us.

Once we are saved, we are His and our past sins are forgiven. It means we release the burden of the past to Jesus; it is no longer ours to bear.

Personally, I much prefer to forget where I came from. My past sins and drug use are no longer a part of me. I am a new creation in Christ, and shame and guilt are two more sins I can do without.

Chris E.

It Is Written

1 Thessalonians 5:16-18
Always be joyful. Never stop praying. Be thankful in all circumstances, for this is God's will for you who belong to Christ Jesus.

Although it is easier said than done, I think that our Creator desires for us to be joyful in spite of our circumstances. No matter how difficult our problems are, if we trust that God has a plan and that all we have to do is have complete faith in His purpose, then in His time, we will witness His mighty power. My desire to pray continually is a work in progress, and day by day, God is allowing me to have a deeper understanding of who He is and to be grateful for what I have today, rather than bitter about what I do not have. We take so many things for granted that others would be so thankful to have. What a shame. What does God owe us?

Mike F.

Beware the Flesh

It is written:
Matthew 5:28
But I say, anyone who even looks at a woman with lust has already committed adultery with her in his heart.

See also: 2 Samuel 11:1-4

As God rehabilitates our minds and bodies, let us not forget the importance of building healthy relationships with members of the opposite sex. We live in a world that glorifies sexual conquest while minimizing the spiritually destructive consequences of sexual promiscuity.

As men of God, we are called to respect and love women and not to lust after them as if they were objects of the flesh (Matt 5:28). Brothers, it is imperative that we rehabilitate our 'passion' and set our sights on things above (Col 3:2). When our desires reflect those of Christ, we will find the pieces of our lives beginning to fit His mold. He will supply the needs in your life. "Take delight in the Lord, and He will give you your heart's desires." (Psalm 37:4).

Josh M.

It Is Written

Jeremiah 29:10-14

This is what the Lord says: "You will be in Babylon for seventy years. But then I will come and do for you all the good things I have promised, and I will bring you home again. For I know the plans I have for you," says the Lord. "They are plans for good and not for disaster, to give you a future and a hope. In those days when you pray, I will listen. If you look for me wholeheartedly, you will find me. I will be found by you," says the Lord. "I will end your captivity and restore your fortunes. I will gather you out of the nations where I sent you and will bring you home again to your own land."

During the first few years of my life up until I was in my mid-twenties, life to me was a joke. I took everything for granted and took credit for everything I accomplished. I knew the Lord and I thought I knew my plans for life. To me it was set in stone. When I turned 25, life took a tragic turn. I went from a guy who thought he had it all to someone who had nothing. I was caught up in ADDICTION. Every day from then until around June of 2012, I had no hope and did not think life would ever amount to anything. That is, until Jeremiah 29:11 really touched my heart and it gave me hope. The Lord tells me that life is not in my control. My future is in His hands. He's not out to harm me. He gives me hope! I know as long as I keep this verse that "is written" in my heart and try to fulfill His mission He has given me, I will have boundless hope.

Matt F.

1 Chronicles 4:10
He was the one who prayed to the God of Israel, "Oh, that you would bless me and expand my territory! Please be with me in all that I do, and keep me from all trouble and pain!" And God granted him his request.

Prayer is intended for repentance, praise, thanks, and intercession. But sometimes I forget to pray for myself. Of course, it is important to not only glorify God in prayer and pray for the needs of others, but God loves His children and wants to bless His children. This prayer by Jabez is about opportunity. An opportunity for a Christian is an opportunity for Christ to shine through Christian lives. When my territory is increased and I step out in faith (out of my comfort zone), God will not only use me for His will, but He will bless me…indeed.

Zack C.

Philippians 2:21
All the others care only for themselves and not for what matters to Jesus Christ.

In life, I get to live for Him and spread the gospel. In death, I get to join Him. So it's a win—win situation and both bring glory to the Father.

Aaron C.

It Is Written

Psalm 40:1-2
I waited patiently for the Lord to help me, and he turned to me and heard my cry. He lifted me out of the pit of despair, out of the mud and the mire. He set my feet on solid ground and steadied me as I walked along.

Waiting patiently on the Lord is hard. I always wanted things to happen right then and there. I used to live life according to my will. I would try to make things happen the way I wanted them to happen. All I did was make a huge mess of my life. Instead of giving it all to God, I used drugs and alcohol to keep from feeling the pain I had caused myself. This didn't work at all. All I did was create more and more pain. The pain was so intense, I couldn't bear it. I remember praying and asking for God to send me an angel. I knew I couldn't do this alone.

God heard my cry. God led me to Freedom Farm where He opened my eyes. He made me realize I didn't need an angel. All I needed was Him. He already sent Jesus Christ here 2,000 years before I was born. I realize now when I prayed this prayer, I was surrendering. I have truly given my life to God and He pulled me out of the pit I was in. He has given me peace, joy, and hope. God is great and He is all I need.

Joshua K.

At this moment I feel just plain hurt, almost sick. As we discussed at the Center, we would almost do anything to avoid any confrontation, or trouble, or do anything that gives me the feeling of letting someone else down, or even worse, letting myself down. All I had to do was deny myself and not smoke for 40 little days. Yeah, it does mean trouble for me if I don't tighten up. I'm feeling really exposed right now and down on myself, partly because I was caught and partly because I really feel bad about what I did. I was not wanting anyone to know. It was more important for me to impress Robbie or you than keeping it real and not lying. I know we mess up; I hope you and Robbie and others don't look down on me. I sincerely apologize for not following the rules and I will do my best to ask God for help and guidance through the rest of my time in the program.

Zack C.

Ephesians 2:8-9
God saved you by His grace when you believed. And you can't take credit for this; it is a gift from God. Salvation is not a reward for the good things we have done, so none of us can boast about it.

For we are saved by grace through faith. These words say that God, through His love, gave us what we do not deserve. We are sanctified by faith in the gospel of Christ Jesus. We cannot be saved by our works or anything we do because the work was done on the cross; and we had nothing to do with that. God has freely given us His gift through redemption. So if we boast, the only thing that we can boast about is Christ Jesus.

Mark A.

Proverbs 3:5-6
Trust in the Lord with all your heart; do not depend on your own understanding. Seek His will in all you do, and He will show you which path to take.

To trust in the Lord with all my heart is not allowing myself to come into play and when it does, to seek Christ. Leaning not on my own understanding is staying out of selfwill and allowing Christ's will to completely take over my life. Complete surrender is not only a part of my walk with Christ but is necessary to have a relationship with Christ.

Zack C.

Philippians 4:19
And this same God who takes care of me will supply all your needs from His glorious riches, which have been given to us in Christ Jesus.

I rest assured that God will supply not just some of our needs, but all of our needs according His riches.